In the Christian Spirit

In the Christian Spirit

Louis Evely

*Translated by Brian
and Marie-Claude Thompson*

Herder and Herder

1969
HERDER AND HERDER NEW YORK
232 Madison Avenue, New York, N.Y. 10016

Original edition: *Une spiritualité laïcs,*
published by the author.

Library of Congress Catalog Card Number: 74–75257

Comp
cc

Contents

	Introduction	9
I.	Poverty	19
II.	The Priesthood of the Laity	31
III.	Work	43
IV.	The Spirituality of Marriage	57
	Homily on the Gospel of the Nuptial Mass	70
	Women and Work	77
V.	Community	87
VI.	Hope	95

In the Christian Spirit

Introduction

Are you attentive to the signs of the times? "Christ said to the multitudes, 'When you see a cloud rising in the west, you say at once, "A shower is coming," and so it happens. And when you see the south wind blowing, you say, "There will be scorching heat"; and it happens. You hypocrites! You know how to interpret the appearance of earth and sky; but why do you not know how to interpret the present times?'" (Luke 12, 54–57).

Are you enthusiastic about your time? Are you watching for the signs, the direction of the action of God, the calls and the inspirations of the Spirit who falls even on the pagans (Acts 10:14), the illuminations of the Word who "enlightens every man coming into the world" (John 1, 9) and whose voice is heard by "every one who is of the truth" (John 18, 37)?

To believe in God is to believe in the salvation of the world. To hope in God is to hope in the salvation of the whole world, as you ask at every Mass. And to love God is to love the world, for we love a God who has so loved the world that he continually sends us towards it.

The Christian today is no longer preoccupied with thoughts of heaven, nor imagines and longs for the life of heaven, nor is he in a hurry to get there. Twenty years ago, in our churches, each Lent, the brief code of Christian life was read: "Kingdoms collapse, empires fall; the only thing which counts is to save one's soul. Before this question, all the others fade away or disappear . . ." Well, this apologetics is without effect nowadays. We dislike being talked to about "saving our souls" and above all about a "future life."

For the Christian does not believe in a future life. The future life is truly the opium of the people. We Christians believe in eternal life, and a moment's reflection suffices to understand that, if it is eternal, it has already begun, it is not future!

Eternal life is right now. We live it here below, and this is why the life of today thrills us, and should thrill us.

"And this is eternal life, that they know you, the only true God, and Jesus Christ whom you have sent" (John 17, 3), the God-man, the incarnate Word. Those to whom this knowledge and this love have given no joy here below will not feel any up above. Everything begins right now, hell and heaven.

In hell, one waits for a future life (hell is paved with good "intentions"), one wishes it all to change. In heaven one wishes it all to last. Are you in heaven, or in hell?

Have you discovered in your life something good enough to want to live of it forever? Do you love anyone, do you love a few people, enough to wish to make them eternal? Do you wish your community, your marriage, to last forever?

I know but one Christian morality: do whatever you want but do something good enough for you to live of it forever. Heaven will not be a long vacation from conjugal or community life, liberation from our marriages and our communities. There is no use in deceiving yourselves about this point. "He" will still be there, "she" will always be there, "they" will come along with us. So we might as well begin at once to get along together forever.

In hell, one wishes to change wife, husband, parents, children, neighbors, brothers and sisters; or, at least, one waits impatiently for them to change. In heaven one loves them enough to love them forever.

Formerly, too, one only appreciated intemporal things. "What is that which is not eternal!" The temporal could only be the object of contempt; it was temporary. What was ideal was immobile.

But today we have learned with Péguy that the supernatural is itself carnal and that the eternal is experienced in the temporal. One no longer believes that action and movement are inferior. Quite to the contrary, one foresees an indefinite evolution, a progress without end. What corresponds, in the creature, to the infinite perfection of God is an indefinite perfectibility. If we were immobilized, we would be shut up in our finitude, our most fundamental tendency would be denied, which is to perfect ourselves indefinitely. The eternity of a creature cannot be identical to the eternity of God, and the resurrection of the body promises us the existence of time even in our heavenly condition.

Finally, the interest of modern man has moved from the religious properly so-called (monks and priests) to fix itself on the laity. Formerly, when a layman had caught a little religion, he would immediately think of withdrawing into a convent or at least of affiliating with a Third Order. Nowadays religious orders are being secularized.

Hermits were replaced by cenobites; the latter are giving way to secular institutions, and we may hope that the twenty-first century will see religious orders of married people! Then the religious will have become completely secular, and the layman completely religious. Then Christ will have brought about his religious revolution: to create worshipers in spirit and in truth who depend neither on locations ("Is it in Jerusalem or in Garizim? in the convent or in the world, that one should worship God?"), nor on clothes, nor on states of life, but who would be perfect even as the heavenly Father is perfect.

For this evolution of our time, which to certain people seems a step backwards, a scandal, a dreadful decadence, corresponds exactly to what Christ did: *he* made heaven come down on earth, the eternal go into the temporal, and the religious into the profane, forever.

Christ desacralized religion, worship, the sacred. But he sacralized man.

He desacralized the temple ("Neither on this mountain, nor in Jerusalem . . ." "I will destroy this temple that is made with hands, and in three days I will build another not made with hands": his body, made of innumerable members); the Sabbath (which is made for man and not man for the Sabbath); the fast (do not put my new wine in your old wineskins); the priest and the levite (a charitable heretic is better than an uncharitable priest); and even worship ("I want mercy and not sacrifice." "If you are offering your gift at the altar, and there remember that your brother has something against you, leave your gift there before the altar and go . . .").

Only one thing is sacred: man. You will be judged, not on your worship, not on your attitude towards God: you will be judged on your attitude towards your neighbor. Read Matthew 7, 21-23: "Not everyone who says to me, 'Lord, Lord,' shall enter the kingdom of heaven . . ." Not even those who prophesy (I suppose that this is aimed at preachers), or cast out demons, or do miracles. We will not be judged on pure "religiosity." Luke says it in an even better way: "When once the householder has risen up and shut the door, you will begin to stand outside and to knock at the door saying, 'Lord, open to us.' He will answer you, 'I do not know where you come from.' Then you will begin to say, 'We ate and drank in your presence . . .'" (We attended Mass every Sunday and went to communion, we perhaps spent some time in adoration or attended evening services), "'. . . and you taught in our streets'" (We heard countless sermons, and we followed retreats . . .), "But he will say, 'I tell you, I do not know where you come from; depart from me, all you workers of iniquity" (Luke 13, 25-27).

One can be saved without "worship." Matthew affirms it in the parable of the last judgment for all those who have loved and served their neighbor without having recognized the Lord. It would be too bad, of course, to realize this economy. It is not what Christ did, whose entire life was worship and thanksgiving to the Father. But it is, nonetheless, possible. Whereas it is impossible to be saved without one's brothers: "You gave me no food, no drink, you did not visit me, welcome me, comfort me . . . Go into the eternal fire."

Every sacrament has substitutes: baptism of blood or of desire, spiritual communion or perfect contrition. But there is no substitute for the love of neighbor. The rich man implores, cries, begs in vain: he who has excommunicated himself from the love of his brother is excommunicated from God forever.

You will not be judged on your love of God in his heaven, but on your love of God in your brother. You have the same relationship with God as you have with your neighbor.

The sacred is no longer comfortably put away in the worship of God; it is spread out in your entire life. We no longer have a religion of temples or priests, a hothouse religion, but a religion of the open air and open spaces, in spirit and in truth, a religion of laymen.

The example of someone like Charles de Foucauld can help us to build this lay spirituality. He may do so powerfully providing that we follow him in his "itinerary," without stopping at the stages beyond which he himself went.

He began his route steeped in a medieval mysticism; mysticism of the crusades, of the pilgrimages to the holy places, of the literal imitation of Christ (with reconstitution of the landscape). The spirituality of Nazareth: to go where he lived, to repeat his gestures, to touch the objects he handled, to kiss the earth he had trod.

But he loved Christ so sincerely, so truly, that he went through this romanticism to reach and create a modern spirituality: the mysticism of the apostolate. He understood that the true Nazareth is not in Palestine (and he left it), but in any place where the Church is small, ignored, obscure, without light or warmth; that the true Nazareth where we should go and work is our parish, our family, our community, our profession, and, particularly, the places where the most underprivileged men, the poor, live and work.

To live Christ's public life is, for us, to preach, to teach, to cure, to build roads and houses, to irrigate deserts.

To participate in Christ's passion is not to go on a pilgrimage to the Mount of Olives, but to support your family, your community, your pastor, to suffer from them with more faith and not to be scandalized at being persecuted like the Lord.

To live the Resurrection is to believe that forgiveness and reconciliations are possible. The Resurrection, for the Church of our time, is the renewal movement. Give it your time and devotion.

Charles de Foucauld understood all this so well that he finally came to renounce momentarily the Real Presence which he so venerated, in order to go and put himself at the service of the Touaregs. He realized that the presence of a man living of Christ was more urgent and more efficacious than the presence of the Host; that the Host in itself does not have the magic action which too many Christians look for in adorations of the holy sacrament. The Host does not emit waves, it is not a power station of beneficial emanations.

He was the emanation, a baptized member of the living, life-giving Christ. He went towards men to bring them Christ living in *his* flesh. "Sacrifices and offerings you have not desired, but a body you have prepared for me . . . Then I said, 'Lo, I have come to do your will, O God'" (Hebrews 10, 5-7).

Modern spirituality contrasts sharply with that medieval spirituality which de Foucauld has helped us to go beyond: a spirituality of enclosure, solitude, contemplation. Saving one's soul: three errors in three words, for it is God who saves us, we have to save the others, and we believe in the resurrection of our body. *Terrena despicere*: to despise earthly things, whereas we are charged with the redemption of the world (Romans 8, 19).

We have passed from a spirituality of detachment to a spirituality of commitment. It is scandalous to be "detached."

I remember an old maid—well, she was at least twenty-six—who was dying. Her confessor was comforting her, preparing her: "My child, renounce everything, abandon this earth, commit everything to the Lord," when the girl, suddenly coming out of her half-coma, said: "Father, I regret nothing and no one." The priest had a human reflex: "That's scandalous," he cried out. And it was true. In twenty-six years she had found nothing to which she could attach herself! And she is still so, for she did not die. She was not worthy of death. What pitiful homage she would have paid to the creator, having found nothing interesting in his work. Her realization of "Love one another!" was "I care for nothing and no one!"

We should be neither attached nor detached: we should be attached rightly. We must love the world in order to save the world. We must believe in the same Father who created the world and who saved the world, and collaborate with him to complete this creation and this redemption.

The vastness of this task is unparalleled.

All family life, all conjugal, professional, national, international, economic, and political life must be thought out again and renewed.

I was recently re-reading the Acts of the Apostles and a sentence struck me: "And with great power the apostles gave their testimony to the resurrection of the Lord Jesus." I imagined wondrous miracles, extraordinary preaching, irrefutable demonstrations. But in the next verse, I read this: "There was not a needy person among them" (Acts 4, 33-34). No one among them was in need of bread, friendship, presence, support, help, care, and attention!

Christ had indeed to be risen among them for them to have thus upset their society, transformed their structures.

If we were to bring about a society in which no one was hungry, hungry for friendship, for health, for understanding, for respect, for culture, we would powerfully bear witness that Christ is risen.

I

Poverty

The great problem of our time is that of mass dehumanization: through hunger, of course, but also, for those who are not hungry, through machines, through machine-work, machine-pleasure, through an economy which puts men at the service of goods and enslaves man to what he possesses.

We will therefore begin our study of lay spirituality by speaking of the beatitudes and particularly of poverty. The words of Christ: "Happy those who are poor!" are at the basis of a restructuring of contemporary society.

It is the role, the function of the word of God to make us poor. "You are already pruned by the word which I have spoken to you" (John 15, 3). Our poverty is born from the exigencies of truth and love, that is to say, of the Gospel: the word of God calls us into question, unsettles us from our ideas and our habits. "When his sheep hear his voice, they move . . ."

The tragedy of the present-day Church is, on the contrary, the inertia of the huge mass of Catholics. They are Christian for reasons of tradition and milieu. They are rich in practices, prejudices, and institutions; they believe in their parents, their teachers, their pastors, but they do not believe in God. The Jews, the contemporaries of Christ, believed in their parents, and they were good parents; in their priests, and they were true priests; in their religion, and it was the right religion of the time. But God was in their midst and they did not believe in him. They had excellent religious structures: synagogues, holy books, practices, levites, a temple, but instead of actively using these structures to discover the God hidden among them, they rested on their structures, they fell asleep in their structures, and they were damned in their excellent religious structures.

We Christians also possess powerful, heavy, manifold religious structures but we are in danger of putting our confidence in them and exempting ourselves from living of them. Where are the Christians for whom the word of God is not only a solid capital, a "deposit of revelation" safely put away in a closet, but an experience: "No man ever spoke to us like this man!"

Richness is death and poverty is life. The poor man is called into question, he asks himself questions, he is unceasingly thrown back into the changing stream of life.

Jesus said, "Truly, truly, I say to you, if any one keeps my word, he will never see death" (John 8, 51). He is living forever under the influence, under the shock, under the percussion of the word of Life. "He who is of God hears the words of God; the reason why you do not hear them is that you are not of God" (John 8, 47). What questioning such a judgment arouses in us! What obligation to live!

Ask yourself the question, "Do I want to become richer and richer or poorer and poorer?" and you will realize that we are still, after two thousand years, vascillating under the shock, the scandal of the beatitudes.

Poverty is so fundamental that it distinguishes between pagans and Christians. Generosity, honesty, righteousness are not the monopoly of the faithful. Unbelievers often precede us on the path of justice, of the socialization of the world, of human promotion, of the liberation of the oppressed . . .

We would be tempted to say of them, "They are Christians without knowing it." But we should not say this, because they do not particularly like it, and also because it may not be true.

Yet there is still one question to ask about them, that of poverty: Do they live these values, which are real, in humility or in pride; in sufficiency and superiority, or in poverty?

Culture and virtue may be obstacles to the kingdom of God, for if one has formed the habit of looking at truth and virtue as a conquest, one is ill-disposed to welcome the gift of God.

Religious Pharisaism is also the vice of the rich: the Pharisee is satisfied with himself, proud of what he has acquired, satisfied with his behavior, possessive of his truth. Let us not say, "I have faith, I have the truth!" The only sign that you have faith is that you are frightened at having so little of it. Besides, it is not you who have faith, it is faith which has you, and seldom to the marrow.

The true question to ask an unbeliever, then, and even a believer, is this: "Is truth for you some*thing* or some*one*?"

If we envisage truth as a thing, it is normal for us to try to conquer it by reasoning, demonstrations, discussions, and to aim at possessing it. But if truth were Someone, our only possible dispositions towards him would be those of welcome, openness, respect, attention, prayer: the dispositions of a poor man.

Nothing seems more sincere than the prayer of the unbeliever: "If you exist, make me know you! Don't let me deceive myself about you, imagining that I know you when I don't. But help me not to shut myself at your approach, pretending not to hear you while I know you already."

Prayer, in our Christian life, corresponds to this "infused" character of grace. It signifies that we are poor, that we have to receive the essential things: faith, love, hope. We understand something as true, we do something good only through grace.

Receptivity and attention are signs and source of all love. As soon as one believes himself exempted from paying attention to his brothers, his spouse, as soon as one no longer expects anything from someone, it means that one no longer loves the other, it means that one treats him as a thing. Attention and expectation define our attitude towards others. To love someone is to hope in him forever (Gabriel Marcel).

The same is true for God. If we are not poor, if we expect nothing of him, if we do not desire to hear him, it is because we have stopped loving him, believing in him.

Of course, one must not fall into the opposite excess and bore him with continuous talk (as well as pious inaction). People who pray all the time remind me of workmen who constantly ask to see the boss. Meanwhile, their work is left unfinished.

The Christian is a poor man, and he must go to the poor. The decisive sign which Christ gives of the authenticity of his mission is that the poor are envangelized (Matthew 11, 5). This sign is related to the "powerful testimony" which the apostles gave to the Resurrection of Christ: there were no longer any needy people among them!

But the difficulty in our time is that no one is poor any longer—that is, no one will admit that he is poor. Today everyone wants to keep up appearances, to stand his ground, to claim his rights and his worth, to seem as if he needs nothing and no one.

Thus, if we are to be apostles of the poor, we must be

poor, we must be so poor ourselves that we call forth people among the poor and the rich alike who recognize themselves as poor. Poverty is contagious, whereas wealth isolates and revolts. The apostle must go towards everyone with the face of the poor man, so that before him everyone will dare take off his mask, and believe that it is possible to be happy and poor, because *he* is happy and poor.

The apostle is a person who has experienced his limits, his indigence, his awful insufficiency, but who has encountered Someone kind enough, loving enough, faithful enough to be able to confide totally in him. Then he can go towards all the others, and invite everyone to recognize and accept his own poverty, because *he* has found what he needs to bear his.

The poor man is therefore truly *magnanimous*: he expects everything from God, he can do everything in him who fortifies him. Nothing that man does surprises him (the evil he can do), nor does anything that God does surprise him (the good he can do). He is not afraid of human weakness, for he knows that "nothing is impossible to God." He is not discouraged by his own faults, for the power of God "is made perfect in weakness" (2 Corinthians 12, 9).

If poverty is above all a relation to God, a religious situation, it is also and essentially a relation to others and, secondarily, a relation to goods.

The poor man is not someone who seeks poverty, who wants to give himself a certificate, a diploma, a medal of poverty. Such acknowledgment would be a subtle sign of wealth. The poor man is above all someone fraternal, who seeks the others, who opens himself to others. He is not so much someone who gives as someone who shares; not so much someone who has a poor home as someone who has an open home.

Poverty as such seldom leads to love; and if you seek it, it will lead you to bitterness and pride. Only love, genuine love, leads always, and soundly, to poverty. We must seek first the kingdom of God (where we are all brothers), and poverty will be given to us as a grace.

The first poverty is to work. Woe to the idle! You know the beatitude of the watchful servant (Luke 13, 37), but do you know the beatitude of the active servant: "Happy is the servant whom his master finds so doing . . ." (Luke 12, 43)?

Do you do something useful?

The Gospel condones neither laziness nor fatalism. Poverty does not consist in confiding in providence, nor in leaving to others the task of supporting you. Of course, there are Martha and Mary, and the parable of the birds of the air and the lilies of the field! But have you understood them correctly?

What the Lord condemns is not work but worry. He does not blame you for being occupied—quite on the contrary, since he makes it a beatitude—but for being preoccupied.

He who is worried, who frets and is anxious, diminishes and finally paralyzes his faculty for work.

It is scandalous to have made of Martha, for centuries, the symbol of the active life. Martha is precisely the opposite of an active person: she is restless.

When our Lord spoke, when the word of God was pronounced, there was obviously but one thing to *do*: to listen to it, to let oneself be penetrated by it, to let oneself be worked, and that is quite a job, I assure you. There is nothing which acts, divests, moves more than the word of God. "My Father acts unceasingly and I act also."

Martha could not take it—she went to relax among her pots and pans. The Lord was too demanding, too tiring. She was worn out with remaining quiet, she had to move a little, to stir, to take a little walk, anything that would put her out of reach of God, out of danger of being too revealed, transformed, worked, of being too hurt. Further, she was unable to bear seeing her sister do what she was incapable of, and she came back to interrupt the Lord in order to agitate her too.

True confidence in providence is to work today without being afraid of tomorrow. Let us recall that it was the lazy servant, the one who did not make his talent productive, who said, "I was afraid . . ." It is in order that you might devote yourself to your task of today that the Lord forbids you to worry about what you will do tomorrow.

So do not worry either about being too poor or about

becoming too rich. The Lord wants you to be free, confident, available, happy.

Poverty is not not-having goods (that is misery, and it is an inhuman state which should be fled and prevented); poverty is above all learning to use goods well.

Each age must invent its own poverty, its own way of being poor. Nowadays a medieval version of poverty ("Giving one's goods to the poor") would evade the main problem: one would merely disburden onto others the care of using goods well.

In a time of technical expansion such as ours, we must know how to use the means which are at our disposal. A machine, theoretically, suppresses machine-like work, mindless work; it creates leisure, and we all need leisure in order to pray, to cultivate ourselves, to reflect, to meet one another, to rest.

The danger of our time is dehumanization. We must make judicious use of all machines in order to remain well balanced and to escape a mechanization of ourselves.

There are two kinds of machines, and therefore two kinds of problems for their utilization: machines of production and machines of pleasure. The problem of poverty is therefore of two kinds: how can we put machines at the service of man; and how can we liberate men who have been put at their service?

Everyone knows that machines of production are de-humanizing. But it is enough to think about it to understand that, finally, the machine is liberating. If, momentarily, it still compels many workers to do mindless work, it is by definition the kind of work which machines rather than men should do. Let us hope that someday we will see as few workers in factories as we now see horses on the streets. Manpower will replace man as horsepower replaced the horse. There will then be only human tasks.

But the more dangerous machine is the machine of pleasure. It threatens all of us more and more. For it moves us towards a leisure that is the very enemy of civilization.

Many people today are slaves of their leisure just as they are slaves of their work. They go from one bondage to another, from chain-work to chain-pleasure. They are condemned to the Sunday movie or prime-time television for life. They are anaesthetized by pleasure; all reflection and all conversation takes place at the surface.

Do not deprive yourself or your children of machines; there is a much more difficult and demanding asceticism to practice in regard to them: learn to use them well. For the machine is especially dangerous for young people. The machine is what exempts them from effort. Yet a child becomes a man only through effort. Nature has pronounced an unbearable sentence on children who do nothing: boredom; but the machine provides the means of doing nothing and yet not being bored!

We must teach our children to use machines but not to depend on them, to make use of them and to do without them, truly to master them.

Let us find better values which exempt us from being rich.

All Christian asceticism is not simply to be obsessed with renunciation, suffering, poverty. It is above all a question of a *preference*: of finding a treasure for which one sells one's goods, a pearl of great value for which one sells off all the others. "Sell what you possess"—this is the renunciation. "Come and follow me"—this is the preference.

For it is not enough to be poor in order to be Christian: one must be happily poor.

As long as you have not found a better value, keep your goods, for that way you will be less of a poison for people. Do not think that you have to "suffer." I have never understood those Christians who want to suffer in order to imitate Christ. Christ did not seek suffering. He hated it and pitied those who were under its burden. I would say that Christ was not interested enough in himself, he did not worry enough about himself, to make himself suffer. He obeyed the Father: he loved others. The nobility of Christ's passion is that it is not a search for suffering, a studious asceticism, but love and commitment: "But I do as the Father has commanded me, so that the world may know that I love the Father" (John 14, 31). Jesus was concerned above all to love his Father, and to love and help save his fellow men; the cross came to him—he had not sought it out.

Poverty leads seldom to love, but love leads surely and soundly to poverty. It will make you happily poor.

The poor man is fraternal: he has an extraordinary capacity for communion, for communication with everyone —he is on their level and does not seek to cut himself off from them. He has found friends with whom he would rather share what he has than enjoy it by himself.

He is free in regard to goods. He has some, but he does not serve them: he uses them and puts them to use.

Death, which is the last impoverishment, the last unsettling, has nothing to take from him, it has no claim on him. The poor man has entered here and now into his eternal beatitude: he is filial forever, he is fraternal forever, he is free forever. Happy the poor man, for he lives in the kingdom of God!

II

The Priesthood of the Laity

The role of the layman in the Church has always been a subordinate but active one: he was an apostle, he was consulted on Church questions, he elected his bishop, he participated in the cult (liturgy means literally "the work of the people," "public works"), he was a priest (it is characteristic that the Greek word *"hiereus,"* which means the priestly function properly so called, in the New Testament and in the apostolic and sub-apostolic fathers always designated either Christ or the faithful, and never the ministers whom we now call "priests." The words "priest" and "bishop" are names of functions: a priest is an elder, and the bishop is a supervisor.)

But clerics have confiscated all the activities of the layman and reduced him to complete passivity. The same phenomenon of abdication or divestment as occurs in corporations took place in the Church: the stockholders, who are the true owners, consider themselves as bondholders, content with cashing in their dividends and leaving the direction and the responsibilities to the administrators.

Let us meditate on this text of Jacques Maritain: "Let laymen only make prosper on earth, through pious foundations, religious, who, in exchange, will earn them Heaven, thus the order will be satisfied. This way of conceiving the humility of the laymen seems to have been quite widespread in the sixteenth and seventeenth centuries." (If it were only limited to them!) "It is thus that the *Catechism Explained to the Faithful* by the Dominican Carranza, then archbishop of Toledo, was condemned by the Spanish Inquisition on the report of the famous theologian, Melchior Cano. He judged completely condemnable the pretention of giving the faithful a religious instruction which befits only priests. He vigorously protested against the reading of the Holy Scriptures in the vernacular . . . and, in his opinion, one of the signs of the coming of the Antichrist was the high frequentation of the sacraments" (*True Humanism*).

Nowadays if you ask a Catholic whether he thinks he is inspired by the Holy Spirit, he will suspect you of making fun of him, and if you speak to him of his priesthood, he will take you for a "radical."

But St. Peter says, "And like living stones be yourselves built into a spiritual house, to be a holy priesthood, to offer spiritual sacrifices . . . But you are a chosen race, a

royal priesthood, a holy nation, God's own people, that
may declare the wonderful deeds of him who called you
of darkness into his marvelous light" (1 Peter 2, 5 and 9

Let us try to define and explain the royal priesthood
the laity.

A Christian is someone who knows that he has been called
who believes in his vocation.

St. Paul said to the Ephesians, "Blessed be God the
Father of our Lord Jesus Christ, who has blessed us with
all the spiritual blessings of heaven in Christ. Before the
world was made, he chose us [elected us: vocation], chose
us in Christ, to be holy and spotless, and to live through
love in his presence, determining that we should become
his adopted sons . . ." (Ephesians 1, 3-5).

What Catholic layman believes himself called by God,
necessary to God, present in the thought of God "before the
world was made," predestined to the praise of his glory?

What most of the faithful lack is a consciousness of their
Christian vocation, and pride in and gratitude for their
baptism.

They live a life which they consider to have no real connection with God and his love, and they try to excuse its
shameful paganism by efforts of prayer, by painful and in-
termittent "religious exercises." They ignore their vocation.
They do not know that God needs them and has mobilized

33

and summoned them for the salvation of the world. A Christian is someone who knows that he is responsible for the salvation of the world. Faith is not above all an intimacy with God, a peaceful friendship with the Lord, but the grasping of the plan of God for the world.

God does not want worshipers, but collaborators! If you marry, do not marry a worshiper; choose someone with whom you will be able to build a home. No doubt you will have moments when you will tell each other the joy of working together, but you will not spend your life worshiping each other; that would not lead you very far and it would be rather monotonous. God too wants you to participate in all that he is and does: his joy, his feasts, but also his work, and all his love.

The morning prayer of a layman is a prayer of pride and thanksgiving: "God has so loved the world that he sent his son (that is me), his daughter (that is me), into this world to save it!"

A Christian is someone who "does Eucharist": who marvels that God chose him, called him, was confident enough in him to take him for his collaborator and associate.

The first prayer of a layman is a prayer of thanksgiving. Do you give thanks? Do you have anything to give thanks for? If not, there is nothing Christian about you.

Most Catholics believe that they were born into such and such a family by chance, that they undertook such and

such studies by chance, married such and such a person by chance, and engendered such and such children by chance.

These people must be given back faith in their Christian vocation within their marriage, their family, their profession. Then they would not be so satisfied with themselves, for they would know that it is not their merits, their luck, their talent but the grace of God which has led them to everything which has happened to them; and they would not be discouraged, for they would tell themselves that he who has called them will also give them all they need to do their work.

God needs them to work in the world, God entrusts to them this work, this neighbor, this wife, these children. They are like the wise and faithful steward whom the master has set over his household to give to each one his portion of food at the proper time. God needed someone to make that man better, to make that woman happy, to raise these children, and he chose you, he entrusted them to you, and you are for them the steward of God.

How many laymen recognize that they are materialized by their work! How many good Christians I know have tried for years to pray ten minutes a day without success. Their is for them only one thing true and real, their conjugal and professional life, which is perfectly similar to that of their neighbors who do not have faith. They regularly try to spend a few minutes a day doing something "religious," but it does not "take hold," it always has to be started again, for their regular life is too impermeable, too heterogeneous to their prayer; and, deep down, they do not like to take out time—ten minutes a day—to pray.

They judge the religious value of their existence by the number of religious exercises they have managed to introduce into it, and they therefore feel perpetually guilty of leading a "religious" life only on the edge of their "real" existence, which is necessarily devoted to other tasks.

A Copernican revolution must be brought about in them: they must stop making their life rotate around their religious exercises, and instead center all their religion on their life.

The true question to ask a Christian is this: Do you love your life? Do you have faith in your work? Do you have respect and love for your existence?

You have no more love and respect for God than you have for your daily work. For you have no more love and respect for God than you have for his will, for the mission he has entrusted to you, and which you alone can fulfill.

Every Sunday at Mass you solemnly affirm that it is right and just, proper and helpful towards salvation always and everywhere to give thanks to God. And afterwards you go back to your mindless existence, to your dull family, to your stupid work, to your mediocre neighborhood, where you have never given thanks.

But if you have a stupid life it is because you have a stupid God! For it is he who calls you to this life, or at least to a love which radiates through any work, any neighborhood, and any kind of life.

Christ would like to enter into your work, your family, your existence, whereas you want to get out, and he would work with so much love, he would live your life with so much faith, he would treat others with so much patience and tenderness, that seeing him you would marvel at the mission he had entrusted to you.

To pray should be above all, of course, to become conscious of this plan and call of God. But a false conception of "religious expression," a widespread conviction that the religious value of a man is measured not by his acts of charity but by his practices of piety, makes possible a multiplication of prayers without any change in one's life.

On the contrary, the consciousness of being called, the pride of being responsible, the intimacy of a collaboration, this is what will put us spontaneously in a state of prayer, multiply our Eucharists, and make us go draw from God the love which he asks us to bear witness to.

Work becomes a prayer when it is accomplished with love and respect, as a mission which God entrusts to us. But work does not exempt us from explicit prayer, quite the contrary; one cannot conceive a genuine collaboration without reciprocal consultation, exchange of advice and services, and from time to time a celebration of the friendship.

We have yet to specify how the work of the laity in the

world can be called sacerdotal. The most sacerdotal act of Christianity is to celebrate the Eucharist, and the layman does this always and everywhere.

The Eucharist is the acknowledgment that we owe everything to God, that God has loved us and anticipated us, called us to existence and filial adoption, and this acknowledgment is expressed through a happy restitution, a consecration to God of all that we have received from him. It is the greatest religious act because it is an act of adoration.

The Christian is charged with putting the world in a state of thanksgiving, in a state of grace, in an act of Eucharist. He is priest of the universe.

But, you will say, the function of the priest is above all to sacrifice. What relation is there between a sacrifice and this Eucharist?

The Eucharist is a sacrifice of praise, a spiritual sacrifice (Romans 1, 9), not a sacrifice of bloody butchery; it is an interior sacrifice which is expressed under the purest and most significant form of your real life: bread and wine.

There is no necessary relation between a sacrifice and an immolation (though, for us sinners, the movement towards God, the return to the source, which should be a happy restitution, is often a painful redressing). St. Augustine says that sacrifice is "all work done to unite us with God in a holy communion." You already understand better, then, the eucharistic meaning of all your life as a layman.

Few words have been so emptied of meaning as the

word "sacrifice." One has become accustomed to making it mean renouncement, destruction, immolation, loss, whereas it means the highest and the happiest act in the world: to make something sacred, to confer an infinite value upon it.

Get into the habit of making these equivalences: to sacrifice, to sanctify, to consecrate, to divinize; all these words mean essentially the same thing, and what is to divinize if not to fill with love?

The true worship which God desires is the worship in spirit and in truth whereby laymen fill their home, their work, and their life with love. "What I want," God says, "is mercy . . ." (that is, a love which goes so far as to remit, to atone for sins) ". . . and not sacrifice" (understood as a "religious action"). Thus we can fully understand the thought of St. Thomas: "The faithful are deputed by their baptism to the worship of God."

In worship, in sacrifice, in Eucharist, we breathe out to others the love breathed in in God; we share with others the bread and the forgiveness which we have received (for the only means of giving these things back to God is to give them to our brothers). This sacrifice, finally, is to be accomplished "always and everywhere."

Such is the spiritual priesthood, the interior sacrifice of which the cultic sacrifice, the clerical sacrifice, is but the sacrament: the sign and the source.

For profound feelings must be expressed, our life must be expressly signified and celebrated, life must be sung, our immense need for praise must be given expression and exalted within a warm and fraternal assembly.

But for the sign to be accomplished worthily, it is obviously necessary that there be something to signify. If the cultic sacrifice is to have meaning, it is first necessary that the life of the faithful have a meaning, a meaning which imperatively demands a celebration of the Eucharist and a song of thanksgiving. If not, there are but vain ceremonies, mere pretenses.

Alas, the Church, which in the beginning used its authority to keep away from the celebration of thanksgiving those who were unworthy (those who had nothing to give thanks for), had, later on, to make the celebration obligatory.

The people came to rejoice by obligation; they came to give thanks under pain of mortal sin!

Perhaps now, the Church, in its reform of the liturgy, ought to suppress of the obligation of Sunday Mass. For religion is something so sacred that only freedom should inspire its acts. Nothing good can come through constraint. Never are "professionals" wanted in our sacrifice of praise —only "amateurs," moved by love.

If the Christian does not live in a state of thanksgiving, if he has nothing to give thanks for, if he does not know he is called, chosen, loved, and made responsible for all those who surround him, there is no place for him at the Eucharist.

All through the Bible, God protests against "sacrifices" without truth, against "worship" without love and justice.

Now if the priest alone "transsubstantiates," all the faithful "celebrate" Mass. The priest says Mass not in his own name, but in the name of the Church, in the name of his community. If the people remain passive, if they do not commit themselves in this action, if they do not entrust the priest with speaking and acting in their name, then the priest celebrates "in a vacuum," and his Mass, no longer being a sign of the people's union with God and their union among themselves, will no longer be the source of such union either.

Christ chose as a symbol of his body, as a sign of his presence: bread. What does bread represent if not man's work?

Well, what kind of bread are we going to consecrate? If this bread which we bring to the altar is our work of the past week, what value, what taste will it have? If it is the bread of our life, what taste does our existence have? It would be terrible for us to bring for consecration a bread of hate and bitterness, or idleness, dishonesty, deceit, much less a bread of injustice or cruelty.

It is with your bread that Christ wants to multiply his, it is your bread, your life, your work, which Christ wants to fill with his love and to give as food to the world.

Yes, Christ is present in the Eucharist, but he is present in a community of faith and love, he becomes present by the

41

gathering of his members. He has given his faithful the power of making him present, of making him visible among them, but through the power of their love, of their faith, of their union.

Yes, the Eucharist makes the Church, but it is first of all the Church which makes the Eucharist.

The true celebration of the Eucharist is the thankful expression of a community called by baptism to bear witness to its Savior; otherwise the Eucharist would no longer be the sign of anything, nor the source of anything.

III

Work

I

Let us clear the ground by answering first a few questions raised by what I have said earlier about work.

The Civilization of Leisure

Man has been enslaved, until now, to dehumanizing or non-humanizing work. Our age is preparing his liberation from this "forced labor": each person will be able one day to choose the work which best suits his needs and goals.

In fifty or a hundred years, the state will freely distribute to each person his minimum living wage, produced by collective automated factories. From then on, men will be

43

able to devote themselves to cultural, craft, educational, medical, artistic, and religious activities.

No doubt there will still be a few tasks necessary, yet of no interest. Since it would be scandalous always to reserve them to the same individuals, a "work service," drawn up along the lines of the military service, will employ all men and women for a few months of their life.

Humanity will finally be able to devote itself . . . to becoming human!

This is the great problem of the future: do we prefer that men remain bent towards the earth or over a machine, growing beets, making slippers or packages, or do we wish for them to run the risk of freedom, to have the chance of becoming men, of thinking, of educating themselves, of creating, of praying?

Monasteries are perhaps institutions with a future: they could again become the great schools of prayer which the world will need so much when it finally has leisure. There is a future, too, for retreats and for preachers, for then men will have time to ponder in their heart the word by God.

Parents will educate their children. What a revolution! Fathers will take interest in their children's studies!

Humanity will awaken to self-respect. A man will no longer be ashamed of doing nothing but becoming more human!

How to Bring About Communion

Christ gave an answer to this question forever: in the most inhuman work possible, on the cross, he believed that love would be stronger than anything.

On the cross, Christ celebrated a divine and human Eucharist. He not only reconciled God with man (in atoning for sin), but he reconciled man with God. He filled his cross with love. He filled the world with love, and this love was so powerful that it came to penetrate the consciousness of those who had witnessed it without understanding it. Enlightened by the Holy Spirit they finally discovered what had happened: that it was God who had loved them and died for them, and that the only sign of God was to love in that way.

If you love in that way, people may not understand it, not appreciate it at the very moment. But later on, the world will know that God manifested himself at that moment. Your work may be a cross. You do not give thanks, in that case, because of the creative, fascinating character of your work, but you give thanks for the extraordinary power of love, faith, and hope which God has permitted you to manifest in it.

The Dechristianization of Work

Another word for alienation is non-attachment. A man is alienated from his family or work if he lacks towards them any feeling of communion or interest. By the same token, a man is religiously alienated if his worship has no bearing on his professional, family, economic, or political life; if he practices a few "devotions" that are abstracted from real life; if he believes that God will accept his prayers even though they are not accompanied by deeds. This kind of separation is not only alienation; it is also a dechristenization.

Suppose that in your parish everyone were to go to Mass, confess, and receive communion. Do you think that their actions would have any effect on the problems of the world: education, leisure, professional morality, conjugal morality, economic life, political life, international life?

And yet Christ said, "You will recognize them by their fruits." He praised those who listen to the word and put it into practice.

But many Christians still believe in the existence of a kind of heavenly bank account in which their invisible merits and silent prayers are the capital of their future life.

Work has long been discredited under the influence of the dominant spirituality of the West: monasticism.

In the Christian tradition, contemplation has been judged

46

far preferable to action (whereas Christianity is "participation" in a God "who acts unceasingly" and who commands us to love one another). Monks had as their great principle "to prefer prayer to the application of all the other precepts," and Dom Jacques Leclercq has only recently defined anew the essence of monasticism: "To spend all one's time, inasfar as possible, in the consciousness of the presence of God" (*Etudes,* 1964). He adds, "The *opus Dei,* the choir prayer, the liturgy, were at the center of monastic life, and this Benedictine conception entirely dominated the piety of the Middle Ages."

St. Ignatius initiated modern spirituality by teaching his followers a permanent prayer which is exercised in action even better than in leisure, because religion does not consist in "thinking of God," or in "loving" him by savoring his intimacy, but rather in accomplishing the works of God and his will.

The essential idea of his order was to recruit men capable of finding the perfection of their interior life in their apostolate, whereas the habits of thought of the sixteenth century hardly allowed dissociating sanctity from contemplation.

He unceasingly reminded them that faithfulness to God demands faithfulness to the work of God. God is not served by love but by the tasks which love makes us undertake and in which we lose ourselves, to be at once purified and transfigured.

St. Ignatius knew that work—study, for example—requires man's entire attention, and he blamed those who divert themselves from it to pray or to mortify themselves. It is through engrossing oneself in one's task that one engrosses oneself in the will of God.

II

There is no vocation more religious than work.

Man was created in the image of God in that he works: "My Father works unceasingly and I am working too" (John 5, 17).

The first commandment of God, given before all the others, is "Fill the earth and subdue it . . . Adam was put in the garden of Eden to till it and keep it" (Genesis 1, 28 and 2, 15). God is a creator and he made man a worker. If he rested on the seventh day of the creation, it was not because he was tired; he had simply found someone who would take charge of the rest.

For God is not paternalistic or clerical: he invites us to collaborate. He does not do everything all by himself, he wants to work with a team, he desires collaborators.

God gave the world to man for man to restore it in a "spiritual sacrifice" which the Eucharist signifies and consummates. Man must put the world in a state, in an act of thanksgiving, he must make of it "a world where justice dwells" and "where people love one another."

When all men—fed, liberated, humanized, evangelized— have something to give thanks for, then there will be such a Eucharist celebrated on the whole earth that this world will pass away.

For the pagan, everything is sacred but man; even a tree, a cow, a monkey are untouchable divinities.

Faith is liberating. For the Christian, only man is sacred, and on all the rest he lays the hand of a master.

Thus the technical capability of man has for us an immediate religious value. When the first astronaut explored the sky, John XXIII sent him a congratulatory telegram: they are realizing a wish of God. The average Christian is surprised by this pontifical intervention in a domain apparently so profane. But in Christianity, nothing should remain profane, everything should be taken in hand by man to make of it an object of Eucharist.

No religion except Christianity has given a religious meaning to work, and that is why all religions lose ground with industrialization. But Christianity should spread and be authenticated by technical progress for it has predicted, invented, and favored it, and recognizes its religious value.

We have defined the layman in this way: someone who takes his temporal task—his work—seriously. So far, then, there have not been many laymen among Christians.

A theology of work and of the laity should teach us to set our hearts on our task, as the very exercise of our religious life. In this way our profession of faith would be expressed in our profession itself.

Usually when we pray we thank God for the redemption but neglect to thank him for the creation. Yet what was restored by the redemption of Christ was the creation of God. God's plan must therefore be carried on, enriched with new vigor, new promise, new certitude, science, philosophy, art, economic and social structures, are pastimes in which one runs the risk of losing one's soul.

Like the redemption, the creation demands our collaboration. The world will evolve only to the degree that we labor at its constant rebirth. For the Church is not the community of the redeemed, the saved, but of the saviors. So there is only one duty and one sanctity: to answer that call of God and to adhere to that redemptive will.

Thus any concern about "saving one's soul" gives way to concern about saving the world. Heaven becomes a hope and a conquest (as well as a gift) instead of the object of pious sentimentality.

There is an odd adage that says, "To love one another is not to look at one another, but to look together in the same direction. This holds true for God as well. Christ did not come to be served, to be worshiped and incensed, but to serve and communicate his zeal until it reaches the whole earth. Religious life is not peaceful intimacy with Christ but the elaboration of God's plan; it is a collaboration in the incarnation (which would have taken place without original sin) and in the redemption.

Theology has immensely exaggerated the seriousness of original sin, to the point of making it a catastrophe which has compromised all history to come.

Let us observe, on the contrary, that sin did not stop, or even distort, "the evolution of creation," and that this evolution proceeds victoriously and restores little by little the consequences of the fault—thanks, to be sure, to a redemption just as original as the sin. Is Paradise at the origin or at the term of history?

As far as our subject is concerned, let us not forget that salvation has always been, and will always be, indivisibly, the work of God and the work of man. "God, who created us without our help, will not save us without our help," theologians say. One may wonder, seeing the extent of human collaboration necessary to make the gift of God bear fruit, whether God creates us without our help; but in the second part of the affirmation the whole theology of work resides in embryo.

Let us describe the states of redemption.

The Redeemer will be born from a woman, and his work, begun through the consent of one of us, will be accomplished with the collaboration of all of us. Docility to grace will always be followed by a progress of nature; and every insubordination will result in regression.

Man will once again be master of nature: he will tame the animal, the soil, the climate. Mechanical inventions will lighten his labor, and his work will again be a humanizing and happy activity, just as it was in paradise when he tilled his garden and "named" the animals.

Woman will see the pains of her pregnancy decrease, and childbirth will become ever more easy, purposeful, spiritualized. Further, she will conceive in freedom. Each conjugal embrace will be an act of mutual love, and each conception will be a voluntary decision. There will no longer be undesired children. Husband and wife will fully assume their human responsibilities.

Relations between the sexes will be transformed as well. Not only will man cease to dominate woman, but the disunity introduced between them by sin will yield to a new unity—the original unity: they will be two in one flesh. The sacrament of marriage will make man and woman equal and inseparable. Faithfulness to the promises and demands of baptism will suppress all separation, subordination, and inequality. "There is neither Jew, nor Greek, there is neither slave nor free, there is neither male nor female" (Galatians 3, 28).

Woman's present inferior status is due in part to the values of our society: male labor is worth money, but properly feminine work such as homemaking and the education of one's children is worth nothing. Further, her inferior status is carried over in the Church where, for example, she is excluded from the priesthood by man-made laws only. When will the acclamation of joy with which Adam welcomed Eve have its place in our Eucharists?

Man is also regaining his preternatural gifts. Through teaching, eugenics, psycho-pedagogy, he will eliminate ignorance, and his medicine will prevent or cure illness. The world is uniting, levelling out, being brought together in solidarity; grace is rejoining what sin had set apart.

Many Christians will lose faith in God because of the wonders of man. "What is God good for anymore," they will ask, "why is he still necessary?"

But God wants only to teach us how to love; and the more powerful man becomes the more he will need to love. For man's progress is his struggle against his limits; it is not a struggle against God, who neither has limits nor imposes them. On the contrary, man-in-progress is realizing the command of God: "Have dominion over everything, subdue everything."

One day man's nature will be fully integrated with God's grace and he will live forever. "The last enemy to be destroyed is death" (1 Corinthians 15, 26).

Life in itself is made to last forever. A man dies only by accident or through medical ignorance. If a man is provided with artificial, miniaturized, and indefinitely replaceable kidneys, lungs, heart, why should he die? If science can find a way to preserve his bodily organs in good health, why should a man die?

One day a man will choose to die. He will cease to maintain himself in life when he decides that he has lived long enough here below, that he has accomplished his task and that he should give way to others.

Christ was the first free man, the first who died freely: "I lay down my life . . . I have power to lay it down, and I have power to take it again." He was the first man who judged that his work was accomplished, and thus committed his spirit into his Father's hands.

You will perhaps say that man's future as I have described it is all conjecture, that there is no certainty that such a future will come to pass. That is true; but on the other hand there is no evidence to the contrary, and therefore we should not act as though there is. It is a pitiable apologetics which makes God triumph in the nothingness of man; which finds in our ignorance, our suffering, and our death the arguments which compel us to believe in God's love and existence. For the Christian, man discovers himself to be the son of God who was molded in the image of his Father; Jesus is the Christian model, and Jesus dominated nature and liberated himself from death. Jesus worked miracles; man must work progress. In the end, man will expect from God only what God has offered—love. He who loves his neighbor and loves God is like God, who is love.

Thus we must not expect God to cure us of our miseries: redeemed man can do it alone. Even if there were no suffering and death, God would still be God—and perhaps it is even true to say that, were there no suffering and no death, there would be more love, for suffering and death cause divisiveness and pain (though we do not deny that they can lead also to greater love).

God has a central place for every man, mortal or not, suffering or not, religious or unbeliever; for every man has a right to love and to hope for a true response.

Religion does not rest above all on thoughts of death or feelings of culpability. A free, loving, joyous religion seeks in God the total justification of its love and its joy in loving.

The true God who revealed himself to us is not a God whose almightiness should frighten or coddle us, but a God whose suffering and love call and respond to our own.

Evolution makes man more and more human, for all man's greatness is his freedom and evolution sets him free. Everything that was imposed, necessary, inevitable when he was primitive gradually becomes an object of reason, choice, and freedom.

Marriage was formerly a family and social institution, it has become a personal decision; it now rests solely on the consent of the partners, and this is why it is at once so fragile and so strong.

For a long time man worked in order to survive—but soon he will be able to work in order to develop himself. Machines, as we have seen, will produce enough for man to be able at last to work mainly at becoming more human.

Even religion, which once was a matter of geography or social class, has become a matter of personal faith.

But man will reach his true liberation when he is able to will his death. He will no longer die like an animal, unwillingly, reluctantly. He will die by choice, by preference, through a need for transcendence. Man's most fundamental impulse is to give himself, to offer himself, to throw himself out of himself, and even out of this dim and relative world, towards Another in whom he can put his confidence.

Let us measure how primitive and blind to our fundamental identity we still are when we discover our difficulty in imagining a man who appreciates, values, and respects life, has lived it fully, and who then turns deliberately towards another mode of existence, who ceases to maintain himself in this life because he desires to know his Lord more closely and wishes to celebrate his passover.

IV

The Spirituality of Marriage

Christianity is a religion of love, of incarnate love, and yet, paradoxically, it does not seem to have fully recognized the meaning and the value of love in marriage.

Is this failure due to the fact that in our civilization a woman has long been regarded more as a piece of property than as a companion? From the very beginning of Christianity, especially in the writings of St. Paul, celibacy was clearly preferred to marriage; with the consequence that it has taken nineteen hundred years for this primary from of the love and union which Christ came to teach to all men to be recognized and appreciated.

We ought to admit right off that in the Christian revelation there are elements which cannot easily be harmonized. On the one hand, what is human and carnal is given new value, consecrated: the Word became flesh, marriage is a sacrament, in Christ there is neither male nor female (Galatians 3, 18).

On the other hand, Christ was conceived in an anormal way; even his birth, according to some theologians, took place "as if he were a sunbeam passing through a window-pane," and Mary and Joseph were not true spouses. Mary kept "the glory of her virginity" (as though there were humiliation in being a mother or a wife).

This kind of thinking has engendered mistrust, if not contempt, for the flesh and for life. We Christians live as though we are latent Jansenists: all that is joy is profane, if not questionable, and all that is life is sin.

For many Christians the immaculate conception is the virginal conception—and a virginal conception is the only immaculate one. If Mary is "without blemish," everybody instinctively understands that it is because she is a virgin.

For contemporaries, Mary's virginity was the indispensable means of implying the divinity of Christ. But for the educated Christians of today it would be infinitely easier to believe that Christ was born from a normal marriage, and we would see nothing in that fact which would offend the grandeur of God, the purity of Mary, or the sanctity of Joseph.

Our time is elaborating a conjugal spirituality which sees marriage as the means of human fulfillment and a vocation to sanctity.

Up until now, religious have modestly kept for themselves

the "states of perfection." But are not conjugal poverty, chastity, and obedience (that is, understanding) as perfecting as the so-called religious states? And is not marriage the apprenticeship and the deepening of love, which is the only perfection? Is not this great sacrament, through which two persons promise to one another a faithful love in Christ, a profession of faith and a vow which are as good as religious consecration?

Is God jealous of what is given to his creatures? God has revealed that what is done to the least of his own is done to himself. The only justification of consecrated celibacy is that it allows the celibate to be more availing to the needs of others; but celibacy does not exclusively reserve the consecrated on to God, for God reserves nothing for himself.

For a long time, too, marriage was strictly subordinated to procreation, as though the personal development of the couple gave way to the benefit of the perpetuation of the species. Today we have seen more clearly that it is the very love of the spouses for one another that is called for in the marriage vow. We no longer distinguish two unequal ends of marriage, but see instead a single, complete end in which love and procreation are harmonized.

A proper understanding of marriage is the most important chapter of a lay spirituality. For it is our love relations with others which determine all our personal and religious values.

If the layman is someone who takes his temporal task seriously, then the temporal and decisive task of the spouses is indeed their conjugal relationship. What will anyone do in society at large if he does not make this first society, which is the foundation of all the others, a happy one? What capacity for love can a person have if he does not even succeed in loving "the flesh of his flesh and the bone of his bone"? Of what benefit is it to bring children into a world which discourages them from loving, for they see that adults, though they may love children as children, fail to love adults as adults?

These failures in love are perhaps no more numerous in our time than before, but they seem more apparent because of the breakdown in our century of social and religious structures. "Appearances" are becoming less and less important.

The important breakthrough in our time regarding adult love is that we have seen its intimate connection with marriage. Today people marry because they love one another. They marry forever because they want to love one another forever.

But if marriage is so closely identified with love, how can marriage subsist when love disappears, and above all how can there be marriage if there was never any love?

Is it moral—is it human—for a man to live with a wife who does not love him? Is it moral for a wife to a prostitute herself to a husband who does not love her? Can a person be asked to accept marriage if he or she does not know what it is to live and love?

How many marriages are no longer anything but prisons? Can such a sacrifice be justified, above all if there are no children, or no longer any children?

The great temptation of infidelity is not pleasure or distraction; it is love. Of course, everything can be put under this name. But what if it is the true name?

No doubt every man between forty and fifty thinks he has discovered his great love because someone young, or simply different, refreshes his worn-out desires.

But it would be of precious little help to husbands in difficulty to suppose that their cases are always identical and their temptations contemptible. It may really happen that a man discovers, at thirty or forty, that he has never loved, that he did not know what it was; that he married through reason, confidence, or sentimentality, to be like everybody else, or to escape from home. And suddenly he encounters the person he should have married, the one who makes him exist, who reveals to him who he is, who gives him the joy of living. Would fidelity be to renounce this love and return to his home?

And yet is it possible for love not to promise beyond the moment, for it not to aim with all its strength to maintain itself living and faithful? Above all must not lovers constantly renew themselves through effort, search, faith, and patience?

To this immense problem conjugal spirituality must work to give sincere and discriminating answers.

First of all there must be an effort at education.

Our seemingly libertine civilization has ignored a genuine sexual liberation in our time. For nothing is closer to a puritan than a libertine. They both lack respect for the flesh. Contemporary eroticism is the direct product of latent puritanism. The old taboos are still so oppressive and arbitrary that they provoke blind revolt.

Another question that must be answered is whether young people today are mature enough to make a decision regarding marriage—mature enough, at the age of 21 to decide that at the age of 60 they will still want to be married to the same person.

If we are to face the problem, must we not accept, not sexual, but quasi-conjugal "experimental marriages" or living arrangements? Must we not revise our idea of what female virginity is, on what it means to be an unwed mother? Above all must we not explore more deeply the various methods of contraception and birth control in the context of a marriage of love?

At present, in Christian doctrine, marriage is the only irremissible sin. A person may fornicate any number of times—but he or she will be forgiven if there is contrition on the sinner's part. But if you marry and later learn that you had made a mistake—well, you may be sorry about it but the Church can do nothing for you. Even if a marriage can be considered as invalid in conscience because of an insufficiency of knowledge or consent, the Church cannot recognize it as such because of lack of evidence. Yet it can hardly be denied that some remarriages seem more authentic than many marriages.

Thus the meaning of religious marriage will have to change: formerly one could count on social pressure to help young people to learn to love one another within a solid institution. Now the sacrament ought to consecrate a matured and tested love.

What is marriage without love? But what is love without marriage? As soon as one is dissociated from the other, inextricable situations are to be found in which only hope (to love someone is to hope in him forever), patience, the refusal to hurt those who need us, can be advised; not to renounce living and loving, but to try to love better, to love in a more just way, to preserve for love its essential role which is to create, to invent, to restore.

Love is a faculty for which everybody believes he has genius, but genius is rare in all orders, and even genius involves much patience and study. Marriage is the school of love. Love is learned or, in any case, deepened through patient application of all our strength, through active fidelity to someone who never ceases to reveal himself and who is always seen as a new, fuller, "different" person.

Spontaneously, love is very selfish, it is the need to be loved, or at best the need to love; it only gradually becomes attention to the good of the other. The sign of initial selfishness is the mutual disappointment: "I expected so much of him . . ." "But he expected so much of you . . ."

Not only are both man and woman selfish, but they are selfish in such different ways that each does not recognize his selfishness in that of the other.

Faith is a doubt overcome; hope, a despair overcome; and love, a refusal, an indifference, a reluctance overcome. A honeymoon lasts as long as both egotisms coincide, that is to say, as long as both feel the same pleasure at being together. But all that while it is impossible to discern whether each one loves the other or only his own pleasure. It is only when pleasure fades away, when contradiction, lassitude, irritation appear, it is precisely the moment when one feels loved no longer that for the first time the opportunity presents itself really to love, to love the other, and not one's own pleasure.

Love is sought and found through crises or, at least, mutations. What kills love is not difficulty, but rather facility. A love which quietly goes to sleep does not wake up. Happy is he whom trial compels to dig down in himself to find resources that he did not know he had.

This is what the episode of the marriage at Cana means allegorically. The spouses experience in the middle of their wedding banquet the insufficiency of their resources, the dulling of their love: only water is left! But the Lord intervenes; there is a call in depth; they discover religious resources, and the second wine is better than the first: the second love of marriage surpasses the first, as much as the heart which knows how to renounce itself, to remain faithful and to give without return, surpasses the heart which knows only how to open itself and to enjoy.

To love someone is to hope in him forever! This means indeed that there is more aspiration than realization, but the aspiration must be idomitable: to love someone who does not love us, or at least who does not love us as we love him, who does not love us as we would like him to love us, to love him until he awakens to the love which calls him (but how long his sleep can be!).

Conjugal love navigates between two reefs: resignation and intolerance. Its rule is always to expect, and never to demand; whereas one will always be tempted either no longer to expect anything, or to expect in demanding: "She has only to . . . He has only to . . ."

The only way to change one's husband or one's wife is still to accept him as he is at the start; for what he needs in order to change is to be loved. To demand that he change in order to be loved is to deprive him of the means of doing so. But not to aspire to and work for his transformation is a resignation which is evil in the one who professes it and humiliating for the one who is its object.

One should not say everything at once, but he must never give up the hope that he will some day be able to say everything.

One may find that communication is easier with other persons, or that understanding comes sooner, or that interests are more natural and spontaneous, yet nonetheless one must persist in wanting to create this kind of situation with one's spouse, and even use what is discovered with others to realize it one day, painfully, with him or her.

One must be lucid, and judge the other as he is, but without condemning him to not growing. One must know that love is created by dint of patience; one must call even without receiving an answer; communicate without finding an echo; try untiringly in spite of failure, for this is what it is to be married. These thousand threads, so fragile and thin, come to constitute the solid bond of marriage!

Marriage is an unconditional surrender. But is not love already that? One deliberately violates in love the law of the morality of affections: love someone if he is worthy of it, and as much as he deserves it. The members of a family love one another well beyond what is reasonable. One is not loved because he is worthy of it: one is loved so well that he has a chance of becoming worthy. If in the family one were to love only because the other deserved it, no one would deserve it and no one would be loved.

Love, marriage, draw from our heart all the courage, all the faith, all the generosity we are capable of. It is their fundamental justification. Nothing would have cost us so much, nothing would have deepened us so much. The conjugal vocation, equally with all others, is contained in the words of the Lord to Peter: "Peter, when you were young, you girded yourself and walked where you would; but when you are old, another will gird you and carry you where you do not wish to go . . ." Another, several others, several little hands have taken our hands and led us where we did not want to go, where we would never have dared, where we would never have thought we were able to go.

According to the sacramental meaning of marriage, the spouses relive, towards one another and towards each of their children, all the love of Christ for this person. Within the narrow walls of a single creature loved and saved, they relive the redemption, they discover what the love of Christ is for this person, they experience how Christ would have become incarnate, would have died, and would have given himself as nourishment for this single being. Through the apprenticeship of an extraordinary, prodigal, unjustified, unbounded love, they learn what the love of Christ is for them and for all people. They participate in the redemption of the world.

Within marriage, a universal love takes form and is nourished. A husband, when all is said and done, loves his wife and remains faithful to her (and a wife to her husband) for the same reasons he would have been faithful to any woman. But this woman alone raised him to this total fidelity.

And parents, when all is said and done, love their children for the same reasons they would have loved any children.

Marriage thus emerges into humanity, and love into charity.

Among the new orientations of the doctrine of marriage, there is, to be sure, the blending between the two aims formerly distinct and hierarchically ranked: conjugal harmony and procreation. There is, too, the equality of men and women in the collaboration of a team. Finally, there is the respect for the flesh: it is no longer a question of "a remedy for concupiscence," but of integrating sexuality into the whole of personal life and of making it a sign and a means of love.

The most crucial problem is that of birth control.

The Church has gone astray in the determination of "techniques": temperature or the calendar which "respect" nature. What is a technique which respects nature? A temporal technique is approved, but a spatial technique is contrary to nature!

Besides, either by luck the technique is efficacious and the couple is in order, even with a mediocre morality; or the technique fails and even a generous and fervent couple is reduced to sin.

We have put so much emphasis on the techniques permitted or not that we have left in the dark the essential which ought to have been recalled: that the union of the spouses is an act of love, and there is nothing more contrary to nature than to do it without love.

The day we discover the technical means of knowing whether a woman is impregnable or not, all conjugal morality will seem to disappear since there will no longer be any restrictions. Everything has been done until now as if we believed that the sanction of a child was the best means of restraining the sexual unbridling of the spouses!

The only role of the Church in this domain as in the others is to preach morality, which is summed up in two prescriptions:

Make of each union of the spouses an act of love with all that such an act involves: attention, true intimacy, preparation, and solemnity.

Realize a reasonable and generous plan of fecundity.

As for the means of realizing this plan, the spouses must choose them with one accord, after having consulted psychologists and doctors who will tell them what techniques are reliable and favor a genuine act of love.

Homily on the Gospel of the Nuptial Mass

Dear friends, the Gospel we have just heard links and traces your love and your marriage back to the infinity of time.

God is going to renew in your favor the oldest gesture in the world, that first revelation of divine tenderness and mercy, that first redemption made before sin, through which he took pity on his creature and gave woman to man and man to woman, forever.

Once again today, God says, "It is not good that the man should be alone!" And once again today, man welcomes woman with this acclamation of joy: "This at last is flesh of my flesh and bone of my bone!"

For a long while Adam had reigned in paradise. He was alone; he was master and he thought he was happy. Everything was in his power and nothing escaped his knowledge.

He organized, planned, invested, administered. Animals rivaled in docility to catch his look and his favor.

The creator had entrusted him with the responsibility of finishing his work and man was conscientiously performing his ministry; he was improving the creation and seeing to the good of all those who were entrusted to him. And man naïvely thought that this would be sufficient to fill his life and his heart.

But the Lord knew man better than man knew himself; he knew that man is simple and rough and continually runs the risk of enslaving himself to his work and forgetting his transcendence. Man accepts willingly to resemble what he does: if he deals with abstractions, he soars far above reality; if he is interested in machines, he becomes mechanized; and if he transforms matter, the latter in turn influences and transforms him.

He had to be completed by a being of dialogue, a being insatiable for love and truth, who would never let him forget the exigency of his greatness.

So God's pity seized man when Adam, for once, stops, forgets about his calculations, his future projects, his worries about productivity, and abandons himself to the dream of his heart, and from the side of the sleeping Adam, God drew Eve.

God inspired Adam with a moment of leisure, a moment of revery and peace, an instant of eternity, and Adam experienced a visitation. His sleep was more fecund than his labors. He went to sleep to dream, and he awakened to life.

He then discovered the emptiness of his heart, that he had always lived in exile, felt an absence, a hunger never satisfied, a thirst never quenched; he discovered that he had lacked the essential and that that was to love and to be capable of suffering.

Woman was born from the side of man, from this wound in his side, not yet healed, which opens him to all the anxiety and suffering of the world. What man lacked was to be wounded in this way, to discover this strange weakness: that he needed another in order to be himself, that he could know himself well, love himself only in this being, at once similar to and different from himself, in whom he could be well pleased.

When God wanted to finish creating man in his image and resemblance, he created him man and woman, that is to say, like himself, incapable of solitude, unfit to be sufficient to himself, completely oriented and projected towards another to whom he gives all that he has and for whom he can invent all the happiness which he sought in vain in himself.

What would man be without this call, without this opening in his side which is woman, without this rending summons, this tireless percussion, this ceaseless provocation to awaken, to think, to love, to create. What would he be without this wound through which all that is best in him springs and bursts forth, all that tenderness, generosity,

72

eagerness, admiration, and innocence hidden within him?

What would Prometheus be without his eagle, but a stealer of fire, an unscrupulous conqueror, a kind of captain of industry: what would he have accomplished but a kind of heavenly burglary, if there were not this suffering which humanizes and ennobles him, this compassion which makes him the brother of those he helps, this eternal wound of his failure or his greatness?

And ultimately, what would God be without his mercy, a blissful, blessed, insensible God, if there were not this humanity clinging to his side (for the Church is born out of the opened side of Christ on the cross, as Eve is born out of the side of Adam asleep under the tree of paradise)? What would God be without this suffering, without this companion to which he bound himself, this spouse who rejoices him as much by what she asks of him as by what she brings him, this humanity—so beautiful and so poor—which unceasingly draws out all the forgiveness and love no one knew he was capable of before we wounded his heart.

Man is made for work, he finds his joy in conquest and invention. He is called to dominate the world, he improves it, sometimes he even beautifies it and makes it capable of nourishing the millions of people to whom the Father could not give daily bread if he did not have collaborators who take his honor in hand and keep his Word. Great is their nobility!

Yes, man humanizes the world, but woman humanizes

man. She teaches him to love, she introduces him into a world of freedom, goodness, and joy; she digs down into his heart in order to arouse tenderness and genius. Thanks to her, man will never be happy, never at rest, never satisfied, but always expecting, seeking, inventing a better happiness.

Ah, Adam's word to his Creator is true: "The woman you gave me, tempted me . . ."—and she continues to tempt man, for better and for worse; she creates him or destroys him. Man will always be whatever the woman he loves makes of him.

Scripture is eternal; man is still trying to close this wound; he seeks, even in the Gospel, even from God, a valid reason for dismissing his wife and finding some kind of peace: "Is it lawful to divorce one's wife for any cause?" (Matthew 19, 3).

Christ tells us that Creator's design and all man's nobility is to keep this wound open: let the wife that God gave you endlessly call you to dialogue, personal communication, fecund uneasiness, renewed and recreated love.

The nobility of woman is that she does not even think, usually, of closing her wound. For man too is a wound and a torment for woman: "Your desire shall be for your husband and he shall rule over you." If man is tempted to stop through satiety (he is so easily contented with himself that he wonders how others could possibly not be!), woman is threatened by discouragement (she wonders where she could find the strength to begin again to speak, to explain, to resume communication, to put forward these demands and these requests which man always finds superfluous!).

Woman must accept to remain a living conscience, a heart on the alert, an uneasy mind, participating in all the suffering of the world, but also a witness to its aspiration, to its hope, to this dimension in us which remains to be humanized. Our inspirations are always equal to our aspirations. Woe to the rich and to those who are satisfied. The Spirit can fill only those who aspire towards him; and the kingdom of God belongs to the poor.

This is why you are inseparable. This is why your marriage will be indissoluble: because you will both find your truth only in your faithfulness to one another.

Woman finds her peace only in man who liberates her by fixing her. From the man she loves, she receives the security and the freedom which she vainly seeks by herself.

And man receives from woman the call, the daring, the fecund exigency which keep him from being satisfied and materialized in his work.

But to fulfill so great a destiny, you will not be alone. You are today surrounded by all those who preceded you in this enterprise and who come to give thanks with you for the commitments which bind them. They rejoice in encouraging you to exchange your vows, and to be led by your touching example to renew theirs.

But above all you come to ask the help and the strength of Christ. He too took a spouse, and he gave himself completely for her, in order to make her shining, without wrinkle or blemish, but holy and immaculate before him. He too entered like you into the bonds of a new and eternal covenant, and every day he gives thanks and blesses his Father for having been able to love in this way, for having known how to give his body, his blood, his life to her whom he loves. He is going to inspire your promises and he will inspire you to fulfill them. He will accompany you along your roads of joy and your ways of sorrow; he will continually refresh your love with his; he promises you reconciliations more beautiful than understandings, and resurrections when no one hopes any longer. And it is through him and in him and with him that you will make every day a Eucharist, a thanksgiving more joyful at each stage of your life, for all this love with which he will have enabled you to love one another.

APPENDIX TWO

Women and Work

The work of married women outside of their home is irresistibly developing and constitutes a progress. Of course, the salary of the head of the family should be sufficient for the wife not to be compelled to work in spite of herself.

But the transformation of the conditions of life makes work outside the home more and more desirable. Women no longer have in their home the creative work they formerly accomplished. In the old days, a home constituted an entire universe: it was a meeting place, a hotel, a restaurant, a "salon" (the equivalent of a newspaper), a hospital, a pharmacy, a hospice, a tailor's shop, a canning factory, a primary and sometimes a secondary school. The organization of daily life, of shopping, of heating, of entertainment, the governing of servants, demanded that women give themselves entirely to all this, but in return it gave them proportionate satisfactions.

Today, men have monopolized women's professions: the couturier, the textile manufacturer, the laundry man, the baker, do what was formerly women's work. In a modern apartment, a woman can, if she is intelligent and well equipped, reduce her housework to a minimum, and the latter has become so mechanical and monotonous that it is often exigible that the husband share it, for the only way of lending it some interest is still to do it together!

Of course, the main mission of a woman remains the organization of the home, and the education of her children. She alone can create the atmosphere of affection, security, and joy which characterizes the "home," and which nothing can replace for her husband and her children.

It will be necessary to create very flexible formulas of part-time work, even if for only a few hours a week. The real difficulty, moreover, will not be a question of time but of preoccupation. The great shortcoming of women is to engross themselves in details and not to be able to do anything half way, to be too conscientious and blindly to apply the principle: "Whatever is worth doing, is worth doing well." The new education of women should keep them from annihilating themselves rapturously in their housework, their baby-bottles, —but also from becoming dizzy with social work and activities.

Another evolution: the average life expectancy is continually increasing. Formerly a woman of fifty dressed in black and prepared herself for death. Today at this age, her children grown and her home reduced, she may hope for another fifteen or twenty years of activity. And rather than being a burden and source of remorse for her children by proving unable to live without them, the greatest service she can do them is not above all to look after her grand-children, but to continue, with her husband, a generous and enterprising married life, to make use for the sake of other children of the qualities acquired by the education of her own, and to put her gifts at the service of the community.

The real problem nowadays is no longer the work of women outside their home—that is practically solved, ex-cept for those behind the times. Rather it is for women, at home as well as outside, to do properly feminine work.

The misfortune of modern women is the same as that of underdeveloped countries. When former colonies become free, they reproduce, in exaggerated form, all the vices of the colonizers.

Since men have "colonized" women for centuries, women have no other vision of their independence than in the servile and sometimes aggressive imitation of their former oppressors. Be it at home or outside, we must avoid having women aspire to become *equal to* men by becoming *like* them.

Now, in spite of appearances, our society is totally mas-culinized. In studies, for example, and above all in graduate studies, women have insinuated themselves into a universe conceived by and for men. And if the organization of these studies dehumanizes men, what havoc it can wreak on a woman's balance.

Here is another example: in a society dominated by money and which too commonly evaluates a man by what he earns, the work of wives and mothers at home is counted for nothing! Male superiority affirms itself brutally and stupidly: the husband earns the living of the couple. "Give me some money . . ." "Again! But I gave you some yesterday. What do you do with it? Do you think I'm made of money?" Any normal woman will feel like a beggar, or a kept woman. Thus a young girl, a young woman, thinks she cannot accede to dignity except by earning her living, no matter what the job. This is scandalous. A wife or a mother should not be compelled to earn money, or to do a man's work.

What is properly feminine work?

Well! (Don't take offense too quickly . . .) I notice that most men I know are happy, satisfied, kind, indulgent, smiling; they have pleasant social shortcomings: they are a little lazy, a little gourmand, slightly given to drink; in short, easy and pleasant to get along with.

And most of their wives are unsatisfied, unhappy, nervous, enervating, agitated, agitating, tormented, tormenting . . .

It would be naïve to deduce from this a praise of the stronger sex!

Men are simple beings, they are easily content with what they have, and above all accept to resemble what they do. If they are in business, they become businessmen; if they deal with money, they become financiers; if they work with machines, they become mechanics; and if they work with animals . . . They mix themselves up with what they do, they like efficiency, they willingly consent to become wheels in a machine; they enjoy not thinking of anything, and experience at times in their work moments of total beatitude when they can do nothing.

But women hate all this; their exigency is terrible: they want everything they do to resemble them! They decorate the places where they live, they want to give them a soul, an atmosphere, flowers, cleanliness. Men live in filth with indifference, if not delight. Women personalize everything they touch. They cannot bear a careless piece of work, an impersonal room, a ready-made dress. Nothing is for them pure means, everything has, everything *is* a value. Every person counts; every person is irreplaceable, incomparable.

Men are made for work; they find their joy in the conquest, the domination, the utilization of the material world.

Women are created to love, to give value to persons; tormented by the need, the call, the search for a true contact with others.

Men humanize the world, and it costs them eight hours of work a day and a little pain and sweat.

But women humanize men, and it costs them all the

hours of their day and night, and all the tears of their heart; and they are never done!

Men tear themselves on brambles and thorns, but women tear themselves to give birth to men. And one does not give birth to one's child or one's husband only once in one's life: they have to be given birth continually, to be made human again, to be made persons again, with whom one can dialogue, converse.

Men materialize and harden themselves unceasingly while struggling and working with matter. They identify themselves with the object they ought to transform and use. Then women call on them, call them back to themselves and to them. Women are the salt of this earth, unceasingly awakening, salting men. That's no fun, for either one . . .

In fact, the real strong sex is the female. Biologically her vitality is far superior. Women are constantly sick but they never die. If a woman wanted to be sure not to become a widow, she would have to marry a man ten years younger than herself. But since men are already so much like children at an equal age, this solution is completely hopeless!

Current ideas, and even philosophers, are full of illusions about women. Men take and women give themselves? Physically, is it not the opposite? It has long been claimed that men were active and women passive. But activity is a pain for men and a joy for women. If, in a house, there is an armchair, you may be sure that the husband sits in it. If you meet a couple with a package, the chances are that the wife is carrying it. Now, do not imagine that the husband ordered his wife to take it and that she obeyed! Nothing is more improbable! It is the wife who told her husband to carry it but, tired of telling him so, of seeing him moving so slowly, going about it so clumsily, with such an obvious unwillingness, she could not stand it and seized the package.

It has long been believed that women were passive because they were receptive. But true receptivity is the most creative activity in the world: to know how to receive, how to understand others, to know how to make others feel at ease, to give them birth, to give value to one's partners, to inspire, to call, to reveal.

Men are sterile beings in comparison with women. What is the paternity of men compared to the maternity of women? Nine months giving life, protecting, nourishing, communicating life, and then an entire life educating, inventing, making men.

Men quietly despise women, because *they* make things, they manufacture socks! *They* work seriously. "You do nothing, you women. You amuse yourselves, you stay home doing little things. We men make shoes, cars, fabrics!" Women only make men! Poor creatures!

Women are the strong sex from the religious point of view too, for God is Father, and women are infinitely more mothers than men are fathers. So they fill churches and retreats! Ask in any Christian milieu why women could

not one day be priests or pastors, and whether Christ, in
not calling them to the priesthood, was taking into account
the sociological conditions of his time or had other motives.
The answers, the amused and disdainful pout of men, and
even more the fright and the contempt of women will reveal
to you the place which feminine values have in our contemporary civilization. But if to be a priest is to exercise a
spiritual paternity, would not women be just as capable of it
as men, and even more so?

Thus the role of women in social relations is to humanize
them, to give birth to men. And the sad thing about our
civilization is that it leads women to make shoes: "I am the
equal of men." But it could even be accepted that women
make shoes if they worked in their factories in a human way
and if they demanded that everybody be treated humanly.

Women have their place everywhere, in unions, in social,
political, professional, family associations, in administrations,
in all the councils of men, but on the condition that they do
not let themselves be masculinized, that they remain themselves.

This does not mean that they are perfect! They have
their own selfishness. But when a woman is selfish, she
is never so all by herself. She is selfish for her marriage,
for her home, or her group. She is the citizen of too small
a country. She believes that only her children are from her
womb, whereas all the children in the world are her orphans
if she does not adopt them and defend them. She believes

that the only man in the world is her husband (let us not be naïve: she has a tendency to believe it . . .), and she does not very well know how to generalize her love.

Even if she does not work outside her home, a woman should see further than her own family.

For any man is valorized by a real woman, as any woman by a real man. "This at last is flesh of my flesh and bone of my bone," Adam cried out with joy, before Eve. "I have at last found her who will make me man!"

Teilhard de Chardin wrote: "Since I began to awaken to myself and to take shape in my own eyes, nothing has developed in me but under the look and the influence of a woman."

V

Community

God speaks to us through his word, but he speaks to us through events too. When the Second Vatican Council wanted to determine its program, it consulted the "signs of the times," that is to say, the signs of the action of God in our world.

One of the most powerful signs of his action is the great movement of solidarity and equality which is reaching all the social classes and all the peoples of the earth.

This is as an answer to Christ's prayer: "That they may be one!" Jesus was going to die "to gather together in one body the children of God who are scattered." God has children everywhere, but they do not recognize one another, they do not love one another. Christ would like to make this common sonship a conscious thing by reuniting his children in the Church.

In fact, in our time, everything is becoming global: economics, science, politics, and even war.

Progress, not to mention the survival of humanity, demands unity. It is the only insurance of peace. Just as national unity puts an end to feudal wars, so peace in the world depends on a unification at all levels: not only economic unification, but also political (a genuine world government) and military (an international army) unification.

We are living in a decisive age; we feel global consciousness awakening in us. We felt as much affected by events taking place in the Middle East or in The Congo as we do by events in our own family. We are at last becoming "catholic," that is to say, responsible for the salvation of the whole world.

This creates a problem of faith: our conscious faith is not prepared, is not at the level of this mutation of the world. Many of us, in face of the increasing rapidity of evolutions and the increasing complexity of problems, have a reaction of fear, like peaceful coastal vessels suddenly thrown out upon the open sea.

Fear is a bad adviser: it invites a person to withdraw into himself, to preserve as long as possible what is threatened with disparition, and to live in nostalgia for the past instead of uniting in order to invent the solutions of the future.

Fear makes one say, "Problems are no longer on a human scale."

On the contrary: problems are at last on a human scale!

It is much more human to have to unite and get along with one another than to each manage all by oneself.

And if all men are henceforth concerned by what happens in the world, this means too that all men have become influential. Throw a stone into the sea, and not a single molecule of water remains in the same place. In the same way, everything that happens in Europe, in Vietnam, in Santo Domingo affects us, everything that happens in the United States resounds on the rest of the world. If the world has influence on us, we have influence on the world.

It is therefore necessary to unite, it is therefore necessary to take others into account. If we isolate ourselves we will perish.

But we must be careful: we must unite not only on a world-wide scale, we must unite at all levels. In order to influence events, and in order simply to survive, in order to be taken into account and respected, we have to create intermediary bodies, groups which will defend themselves intelligently, that is to say, while respecting the interests of others.

The isolated individual is condemned. The man who is alone, nowadays, is incapable of being well informed, of judging, of reacting. We have become, without noticing it, citizens of the world. Christians ought to have the joy and the courage to commit themselves to this evolution with faith.

The world needs all kinds of new structures (the

U.N., NATO, the Common Market, the Campaign against Hunger). It is the task of Christians to invent these structures and to commit themselves to them in order that these structures respect persons and natural diversities.

Let us recall what we said earlier about modern asceticism: it is no longer fasting, flagellating oneself, depriving oneself of sleep or meat, but getting out of one's individualism, participating in professional, educational, religious, economic groups and taking active part in their weekly meetings!

The worst sin is the sin of omission: not to commit oneself, not to help others, not to ask their help. It is difficult to feel guilt for this sin because it is such an unnoticeable one.

For two thousand years Christ has said to us, "Love one another!" "Do unto others as you would have them do unto you!" He proposes to us a kind of union in love and justice in which everyone will be much more alive, much more himself, because of all the others.

Alas, Christianity—a community of love—has in practice become a haven of individualism. Christians live for themselves and have their own brand of faith. Our churches are really rows of pews, and people in one pew feel no relation with people in another pew. Everyone for himself—and God for all! Christ would like to pronounce the words of the consecration—"This is my body"—not so much on bread, if it were not the means of transforming us into his body. Christ would like to be able to say of us at the end of the Eucharist, "They are my body. See how they love one another. See how I have taught them to unite and help one another."

Jesus promised the conversion of the world, not if we love God (this anyone can claim, and no one can verify), but if we realize the miracle, exceedingly rare but unquestionable, of loving one another!

People do not understand the meaning of Sunday Mass. The Father has only one desire: that they love one another, that they be united! And everyone thinks that he pleases Him by coming to unite individually with Him!

But whoever claims he loves God whom he does not see, St. John says, and who does not love his brother whom he sees, is a liar. He who pretends to unite with God whom he does not see, and who does not unite with his brother whom he sees, is a liar.

When from heaven the Father contemplates an assembly of Christians, he must shake his head and say to himself, "I've completely failed with them! I begged them to understand one another, to unite, to help one another, to fraternize, and *they* isolate themselves from one another in order to communicate better with me!"

Look in the Gospel for a passage in which God asks us to love *him*. You will not find any, except in two passages recalling the Old Testament, in which Christ in fact affirms the identity of the second commandment with the first. Everywhere in the New Testament, when it is a question

91

of love, fraternal charity is what is meant. Let us recall a few passages: "For the whole law is fulfilled in one word, 'You shall love your neighbor as yourself'" (Galatians 5, 14). "Bear one another's burdens, and so fulfill the law of Christ" (Galatians 6, 2). "Love is the fulfilling of the law" (Romans 13, 10). "Above all hold unfailing your love for one another" (1 Peter 4, 8). "If you really fulfill the royal law, according to the Scripture 'You shall love your neighbor as yourself,' you do well" (James 2, 8).

The whole revelation of the prophets and of Christ is to associate and finally to coalesce the love of God and the love of men.

Already from the human point of view, all education is a progressive awareness of our relations to the world. Without relation, there is no development. The baby begins by discovering his relation to his mother, then he perceives his father, his family. As he grows, the field of his relations widens: neighborhood, school, city or town. An adult has become aware of innumerable interdependencies.

Religion is a total awareness: we depend on God and on one another. The opposite of religion is isolation: the damned are totally separated.

To say, "Politics doesn't interest me," is an irreligious act; it is the refusal to become aware of our responsibility towards others.

Christ is realistic, he tells us: one judges the tree by its fruits.

So let us ask ourselves what we should think of ourselves if we judge ourselves on our relation to others. Do we go towards others? Do others dare come to us? Are we asked for advice, a favor, a loan, help?

Have we found the friends with whom we prefer to share all that we have rather than enjoying it all by ourselves.

Have we discovered the joy of working as a team?

It is impossible to live one's religion all by onself! Outside the Church, that is, outside a group of adults who love one another and get along with one another, there is no salvation!

There is no living faith for us, for our children, for those who surround us, if we do not constitute this miracle: a true Church, a group of people who go beyond all differences of education, culture, social class, money, or origin, because they have discovered a love which gathers them together and rejoices them.

The world will convert to God only if it encounters a true Church.

Apologetics used to begin by proving the existence of God, then the mission of Christ, that he had founded a Church, and finally, what the means of recognizing it were.

This no longer takes any hold whatsoever on our contemporaries. They hate demonstrations, reasoning, arguments. They have suffered too much from propaganda; everything has been proved to them and then refuted. They have been fascists and Nazis, and then denazified; they have been communists, and destalinized; they thought that Latin was the sacred language of the Church and that to go to communion without having fasted was a terrible mortal sin, and now they are compelled to believe the contrary.

So modern men no longer trust anything but experience. Much rather than having the Church prove anything to them, they want to experience it! They are like St. Thomas: they want to see and to touch. They want to find an open heart, open hands, a fraternal, sincere, welcoming love. They want to touch Christ resurrected in the community of his members, Christ living in the love of a few brothers. The world would be sensible to that sign: that God's love becomes living and visible through that of a true Church.

VI

Hope

Christians are, or ought to be, the hope of the world. You have to spread throughout the world the good news: not that one has to go to Mass on Sunday under pain of mortal sin, but the surprising message that God loves us, that God loves and will save the world, that he will do great things in the poverty of his servants.

To believe in God is to believe in the salvation of the world. The paradox of our time is that those who believe in God do not believe in the salvation of the world, and those who believe in the future of the world do not believe in God.

Christians believe in "the end of the world," they expect the final catastrophe, the punishment of others.

Atheists in their turn invent doctrines of salvation, try to give a meaning to life, work, the future of men, and refuse to believe in God because Christians believe in him and take no interest in the world.

All ignore the true God: he who has so loved the world! But which is the more culpable ignorance?

To love God is to love the world. To love God passionately is to love the world passionately. To hope in God is to hope for the salvation of the world.

I often say to myself that, in our religion, God must feel very much alone: for is there anyone besides God who believes in the salvation of the world? God seeks among us sons and daughters who resemble him enough, who love the world enough that he could send them into the world to save it.

Yet Christians prefer to remain among themselves, in their "good Catholic milieux." But a "Catholic" milieu is a contradiction in terms. The Lord Jesus belonged to a "good milieu"; he was from a good family, up above, a very respectable family. But he left his milieu and came to lose himself in the midst of people like us. He saved the world only by leaving his milieu.

St. Peter said to the Christians, "Always be prepared to make a defense to anyone who calls you to account for the hope that is in you."

What hope is in you? What good news do you bring to the world? St. Paul said the pagans were "those who have no hope," and defined the Christians as "those who expect, who hope for His coming."

What do you expect? What do you hope for?

The capital question of our time is perhaps the following: "How do you imagine the end of the world?"

Do you believe that God, at the end of time, will bring us to some prefabricated paradise that he has prepared? Or that he invites us to build it with his help?

Do you believe that the end of the world will be a catastrophe or a completion?

Do you believe that God will interrupt the course of centuries at an arbitrarily chosen moment, independent of our efforts, when he judges that our life has lasted long enough? Or that this world will never end if we do not bring it to completion?

Do you believe that heaven will be completely different from earth? Or that one day the kingdom of God will come and that his will shall be done "on earth as it is in heaven"?

Do you believe in the resurrection of the flesh, and that the whole creation—plants, stars, animals—is waiting with eager desire to participate in our redemption?

Well, confronted with these questions, the Christian usually remains perplexed, He is not prepared; he has not been taught the answers; he does not know what he hopes for; he is not ready to give account of the hope which is in him!

The Christian ought to be the light of the world and the hope of a humanity in despair.

There is a crisis of hope because we are in a period of mutation. We have passed at once from the flint age to the atomic age, that is, from the age of relative arms (flint axes, machine-guns, and TNT bombs are arms of the same kind) to that of absolute arms: those which can destroy humanity.

Scientists tell us that during the next twenty years, humanity will realize more technical and scientific progress than in all the thousands of years gone by.

The rapidity of the evolution of ideas and events becomes vertiginous. We can see this quickness of pace even in the Church.

Humanity is reaching adult age. An adolescent becomes a man when he has found what is worth living for and what is worth dying for.

Humanity, capable now for the first time of committing suicide, a humanity no longer "condemned to live," is called upon to find out what it is living for, and whether life is worthwhile living.

Our means have become gigantic. So the problem of ends is posed in an imperious way. A man who has no shoes, no bread, no home, is a man full of hope: he thinks that everything will be fine when he is clothed, shoed, fed, sheltered. He has an aim in life.

But the man shoed and fed is a man in despair if he finds no use for his widened faculties.

Humanity today knows that it is capable of almost anything. But it ignores the what for of it all, the where it is going towards, the what of its future.

The idea of "God is dead" in the consciousness of most of our contemporaries sets them free, but their freedom frightens them.

For a long time our dependence towards nature was the education and the experience of our dependence towards God. God was thus a kind of intimidating and protective policeman. His power made up for our deficiencies; one came to beg small favors of him; one was afraid of him, and this kept one in the straight and narrow. But when man mastered nature, there was no longer any need to be dependent on God.

Humanity, having lost its false God, has itself become lost. It is freed but anxious. Before, it was in peace: everything depended on God. Now, it has just learned that everything depends on itself. Even to kill itself, even to disappear!

Men still ignore the God of Jesus Christ. Jesus, two thousand years ago, revealed the God of modern times: a God who is not intimidating, not frightening, who loves and forgives. He is not protective either: it is no use asking the Crucified for aid in passing one's exams or in finding a husband or wife. God tells us, "You must be strong with my strength and joyful with my joy, for I have nothing else to give you." God is poor! Of the Crucified we can ask only one thing: That we love and suffer like him.

This God does not recede with the progress of man. On the contrary, the more powerful man becomes, the more he will need love. The longer man lives (and it is possible that he may conquer death!), the more he will have to learn how to love. If I have only twenty or thirty years still to live, I can resign myself to remaining as I am: hard, selfish, solitary, insufferable for myself and for others. But if I am to live forever, I must absolutely change!

The modern world is a land favorable to true evangelization.

But in face of the importance and the rapidity of man's progress, in face of the revelation of human power and the powerlessness of God (God has wanted to be only love and to act only through grace: he proposes himself, he does not impose himself; he respects man's freedom and wants him to do "greater things than he himself has done"), our instinctive reaction is fear, nostalgia for the past, conservatism.

We live still in our own personal dimension. Our hope has not yet broadened and adapted itself to the dimensions of the world.

The hope of Christ is on the dimension of the world: "You will bear witness to me in Jerusalem, in all Judea and Samaria, and to the ends of the earth."

Mary lived on a world scale. She was a modern lay Christian, she lived for the salvation of the whole world; she is a universal Mother.

But we Christians too often live for our little individual salvation, that of our family, our class, our country.

The world will convert to anyone who takes an interest in it, to anyone who loves it, who believes in it enough to promise it the greatest hope.

Socialism, Nazism, Marxism, fascism, communism are promises of hope, confused presentiments that the world must unite, awkward uprisings towards that unity to which everyone aspires and which no one can realize.

Christ promised us that unity, and it is to us Christians that he confided the work of converting the world; this we shall do if we love one another.

But too often, as I have said, Christians, instead of being uplifted by this hope, are afraid of the future. They regard the end of the world as a thing of terror. They fear the return of their Lord!

Let us read the way St. Paul saw the future: "I want you to understand this mystery, brethren: a hardening has come upon part of Israel, until the full number of the Gentiles comes in, and so all Israel will be saved . . ." (Romans 11, 25-26). Now compare this vision with your own!

The world needs to hope in order to live, in order to go on living. It will convert to whoever promises it the best, the greatest hope. And this hope, it seems to me, must be characterized by three conditions.

First, it must not be individualistic. One of the signs of our time is solidarity. The world feels itself becoming one. A planetary consciousness is taking form among men. Redemption, therefore, is to be something fraternal and even cosmic. The Church, as the Second Vatican Council taught, is to be an instrument working for the salvation of the whole world: not just all Catholics, all Christians, but Jews, Moslems, athiests—every man and woman. This is our hope and our prayer.

We do not, in fact, have to believe that anyone who ever lived has been damned by our Lord to hell. The Church has canonized men, but it has never decreed that anyone was damned.

There is a hell—its existence is an expression of God's respect for our freedom. Without hell, heaven would be a kind of concentration camp to which all men were destined to go. But God will respect for all eternity the will of man. Everyone will go where his treasure and his heart are. God punishes and damns no one. Do you think that the damned desire God and that God rejects them? This is atheism! Or do you think that God loves the damned and that they refuse him? This is Christianity!

God is love, he loves everything that he has created. He loves the damned. It is the damned who do not love God.

Is there anyone in hell? There is no revealed answer to this question, for it depends on us: it falls on us to give the answer. Redemption is still at work. Love and prayer circulate in space and time. Anything or anyone that you love, you can save. Your capacity to redeem is your capacity to love. We must not be resigned to the loss of anyone!

A second characteristic of our hope is that it must not be idealistic.

Christ is the Lord of the *whole* creation. Let us not, then, be so concerned with saving only our soul. This kind of attitude mutilates and diminishes us. We Christians believe in the resurrection of the body. Let us not pretend that we are or will become something like an angel. Like us rather be like God: who became man! If our bodies become eternal, our "biosphere," or the world which surrounds us in our thinking and action, will of necessity become eternal too. Let us not tire of reading and meditating on the words of St. Paul: "The creation waits with eager longing for the revealing of the sons of God; for the creation was subjected to futility . . . by the will of him who subjected it in hope, because the creation itself will be set free from its bondage to decay and obtain the glorious liberty of the children of God. We know that the whole creation has been groaning in travail . . ." (Romans 8, 19-22).

We are responsible for the salvation of the whole world. We must love this world enough to make it participate in our eternity. Our work will be consecrated. We are in charge of bringing the universe to the point of maturity in which it will fulfill the ambitions of the Creator.

Many people believe that heavenly happiness will be disincarnate, a kind of ecstasy, uninterrupted contemplation, a suspension of our sensory faculties. But the risen Christ, so human, so natural, so ready to serve, tells us that we can be completely united to God and still be fully man, that divinization does not dehumanize, and that our religious future will be to become more human, more loving, more natural, and, no doubt, more creative and industrious!

Heaven will perhaps take place here below, when we have made the world ready.

Do you live on the dimensions of this task?

I have defined the layman: someone who takes his temporal task seriously, who does something eternal in temporal things, who believes that God entrusts the world and his brothers to him, that he must bring them to the point of eternization.

Is your love on the dimension of the world? Do you really want to save it?

Its salvation depends on you.

The world may end in atomic catastrophe, if you lose faith and courage. But it can also end in apotheosis.

Be careful to understand correctly the seemingly sinister prophecies about the end of the world!

The catastrophe, the end of the world, that which you fear, has already taken place. The worst is over. The most terrible event in the history of the world, "the abomination of desolation," "the great tribulation such as has not been from the beginning of the world until now, and *never will be*" (Matthew 24, 21), is behind us: it is the death of Christ. We will never do worse. The death of Christ marked the end of a world. All the signs of the end of the world occurred at the crucifixion: the earth trembled, the sun darkened, the dead rose, the peoples, through the centurion's voice, beat their breast saying, "This was the son of God!"

And as Christ had said: his generation did not pass away before all that he had announced had happened!

At present we are in the glorious phase of the kingdom of God. The risen Christ sends his messenger angels (they are you), his militants, his apostles, to gather the chosen from the four corners of the earth. Our time is that of the Church, of the construction of the kingdom, of missionary expansion. We are busy building the definitive universe.

Finally, our hope must not be paternalistic. Salvation will not be achieved by God himself. God is our Father, but he is not paternalistic.

Salvation has always been, indivisibly, the gift of God and the work of man. Creation is the work of God, but man completes and improves it.

If we were to judge God on the creation at its beginning or even now in its developing period, we would find that he has nothing to be so proud about! There is too much misery, hunger, ignorance, there are too many misfortunes, accidents, catastrophes. But God gave to the world an invincible hope and he calls collaborators—they are you— whom he trusts to restore and complete his work.

The saints—that is, the doctors, the teachers, the engineers, the nurses, the apostles of all kinds—will justify God on the last day, saying, "Look what he gave us the capacity to do!"

The liberation from Egypt was a gift of God, but the work of man. The Hebrews certainly learned this during their forty years of struggle in the desert! And the Promised Land "flowing with milk and honey" was a gift of God but also a conquest, and they had to suffer, to bruise themselves, to wear themselves out in order to produce a little milk and a little honey.

In the same way, "the new earth and the new heaven" announced in the Book of Revelations are a promise of God but they are also a call to the invention, the work, and the generosity of man.

In the last century, Catholics let themselves be surpassed in the understanding of the Bible by Protestants and unbelievers, and went on maintaining for a long time that God created the world with the stroke of a magic wand, in six days, even with buried fossils to lead future scholars astray.

Nowadays even our manuals of religion explain that evolution manifests God's wisdom and power much better than an instantaneous creation.

But they always represent the parousia as an arbitrary and exclusive decision of God. They think that the world will end by some unforeseeable intervention of the Lord who will cross out our practice pages, sweep away our sketches, interrupt our exercises, and bring down, brand new, fresh, prefabricated, the "paradise of our forefathers."

But if by chance—(I do not say that it is certain, for revelation is not clear on this matter; I say only that it is possible, and that one should not affirm the contrary as if it were a matter of faith)—God were counting on us to build this new world under the inspiration of his grace and by means of the love he has communicated to us for our brothers, what an error it would be to elude his expectation while claiming to confide in him!

We ask of God what we, with his help, must do ourselves: he created an organism of redemption, the Church, and it is responsible for his work.

Perhaps we are, on a scale of millions of years, the first Christians, the first to perceive (oh, so timidly) the real dimensions of the redemption—the first above all to feel the imperious exigency of collective salvation, which is something so much more important and more exalting than our personal salvation.

Bad religion has always favored escape, passivity, irresponsibility. By dint of fixing one's eyes on heaven above, one does not see what takes place on earth here below.

The upward-looking must come to an understanding with the forward-looking.

We believe that our God (up above) calls us to go forward. Our faith in an absolute does not immobilize us in contemplation, but invites us to discover him according to our means of creating a world inspired by his love: a world where justice dwells and where people love one another.

I have said it often enough: the Christian does not believe in a life to come, but in an eternal life. His heaven has begun here below; it begins and grows as his love grows. He applies himself with all his might to his temporal tasks, but with a love which he knows to be divine, immediate, eternizing. He expects nothing, he tries only to give more of himself and to love better what he loves already. He is ready to die at any moment without anguish, because he knows that he will continue to do for eternity what he has already begun to do. He is totally of the moment and therefore totally of eternity. He is completely occupied with men, but with the very love of God. He goes forward with all his strength, but with inspiration given to him from above.